Steve Jobs

Steve Goldsworthy

www.openlightbox.com

Step 1

Go to www.openlightbox.com

Step 2

Enter this unique code

BKIPXIJKO

Step 3

Explore your interactive eBook!

CONTENTS

AV2 is optimized for use on any device

Your interactive eBook comes with...

Contents
Browse a live contents page to easily navigate through resources

Audio
Listen to sections of the book read aloud

Videos
Watch informative video clips

Weblinks
Gain additional information for research

Slideshows
View images and captions

Try This!
Complete activities and hands-on experiments

Key Words
Study vocabulary, and complete a matching word activity

Quizzes
Test your knowledge

Share
Share titles within your Learning Management System (LMS) or Library Circulation System

Citation
Create bibliographical references following the Chicago Manual of Style

This title is part of our AV2 digital subscription

1-Year K–5 Subscription
ISBN 978-1-7911-3320-7

Access hundreds of AV2 titles with our digital subscription.
Sign up for a FREE trial at **www.openlightbox.com/trial**

HISTORY MAKERS:
PAST AND PRESENT

Steve Jobs

Contents

Who Was Steve Jobs?

S teve Jobs was the co-founder and **chief executive officer (CEO)** of one of the most successful companies of all time, Apple Inc. Apple is responsible for the development of the computer known as the Macintosh, or Mac. The company also created the iPhone, the iPad, and the Apple Watch. As an inventor, Steve held more than 230 patents, or exclusive rights, to equipment such as computers, portable devices, keyboards, and computer mouses. Steve was also the CEO of Pixar Animation Studios, the movie company that produced such hits as *Toy Story*, *Up*, and *Brave*.

In August 2011, health problems forced Steve to step down as Apple's CEO. He had been battling cancer for eight years. However, Steve continued to work with Apple until his death on October 5, 2011.

Apple opened its first retail store on May 19, 2001, in McLean, Virginia. Today, there are more than 500 Apple stores in at least 25 different countries, including Italy, Thailand, and France.

Growing Up

Steven Paul Jobs was born in San Francisco, California, on February 24, 1955. Shortly after his birth, he was **adopted** by Paul and Clara Jobs. They raised Steve in the city of Cupertino. The city is in a part of California known as Silicon Valley. This area is the birthplace of many of the world's leading technology companies. Today, several computer-industry companies, such as Google, have their main offices there.

Growing up, Steve was an average student. This changed when his family moved to the city of Los Altos. Many of his new neighbors were working in the emerging field of electronics. Steve began talking to them about their work. Soon, he was using home electronics kits to make various devices.

Stephen Wozniak and Steve Jobs were part of the Homebrew Computer Club. This group met between 1975 and 1986 to trade computer parts and learn more about technology.

In high school, Steve met another student named Stephen Wozniak. Stephen was known as Woz to his friends. Woz was building a **circuit board** and was impressed that Steve understood how it worked. Soon, the two boys were working together on various electronics projects. Over time, Steve's fascination with electronics led him to a job at Atari, one of the first video game companies.

Map of the United States

CANADA

Pacific
Ocean

UNITED STATES

Atlantic
Ocean

MEXICO

SCALE

Hawaii

150 miles
150 km

Alaska

500 miles
500 km

California

500 miles
500 kilometers

LEGEND ■ California ■ United States ■ Other Countries
■ Water ---- International Border ---- State Border

California Symbols

TREE
California
Redwood

BIRD
California
Valley Quail

Flower
California Poppy

California FACTS

California is the most **populated** U.S. state, with about **39 million residents**.

With an area of **163,695 square miles** (423,968 sq. km), California is the **third largest U.S. state**, after Alaska and Texas.

Close to half of the **fruits and vegetables** produced in the United States **are grown in California**.

Practice Makes Perfect

In the early 1970s, computing was still a new science. There were companies using computers, but these machines took up entire rooms and were very complicated to run. Steve Jobs had a vision. He saw a future in which ordinary people would have their own computers. They could work on computers in their offices and use them at home. They could even take their computers with them. These computers would help make people's lives easier.

Other people had similar ideas and were working toward making computers smaller and easier to use. Computer technology changed in 1974 when Intel Corporation introduced the 8080 **microprocessor**. It was the first microprocessor to be both affordable and powerful enough for use in a personal computer.

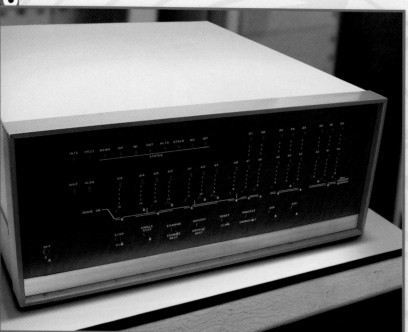

The Altair 8800, one of the first personal computers, was built around the Intel 8080 microprocessor. The computer was unveiled on the cover of *Popular Electronics* magazine and called the "World's First Minicomputer Kit to Rival Commercial Models."

Microprocessor technology helped Stephen Wozniak create a new type of personal computer. It was the first to directly connect the keyboard and screen to the computer itself. In earlier types, users had to access the computer remotely through a terminal.

When Steve saw what his friend had done, he knew instantly that this was the technology his ideas had been waiting for. He set to work with Woz, building and selling the new computers. Recalling a job he once had at an apple orchard, Steve came up with the name Apple for their company.

Jobs FACTS

In California, **October 16** is known as **Steve Jobs Day**.

By the age of **23**, Steve was **worth more than $1,000,000**.

Steve owned approximately **100** of his signature **black turtleneck sweaters**.

Stephen Wozniak and Steve Jobs started selling the Apple I to customers in 1976.

Key Events

In 1977, Steve and his company developed the Apple II, the first color computer. It had sound and **high-resolution graphics.** At about this time, Steve met businessman Mike Markkula. Mike joined Apple with the aim of taking the company to the top of the computer world. He started a **marketing campaign** to advertise the Apple II. He hired people to create a company **logo** and design a case for the Apple II. As a result of his marketing efforts, the Apple II began to sell very well. Apple went from selling 2,500 computers in 1977 to more than 35,000 in 1979. Steve became a multimillionaire during these two years.

The Apple II was released in 1977. More than five million of these computers were produced by the time they were discontinued in 1993.

In 1986, Steve acquired the computer graphics division of another company. He named his new company Pixar. The company used computers to make animated films. Its work caught the attention of Disney Studios. The two companies worked together to produce the movie *Toy Story* in 1995. In the following years, Pixar went on to produce *Finding Nemo, Cars*, and *WALL-E*.

Thoughts from Steve

Steve worked hard to achieve his success and experienced many challenges along the way. Here are some of his comments about his work and life.

Steve knew the value of quality.
"Be a yardstick of quality. Some people aren't used to an environment where excellence is expected."

Steve and Apple put great emphasis on the design of their products.
"Design is not just what it looks like and feels like. Design is how it works."

Steve realized that everyone makes mistakes.
"…sometimes when you innovate, you make mistakes. It is best to admit them quickly, and get on with improving your other **innovations**."

To be successful, Steve believed that people must always strive to do things in a new and better way.
"Innovation distinguishes a leader from a follower."

Steve talked about staying a step ahead.
"You can't just ask customers what they want and then try to give that to them. By the time you get it built, they'll want something new."

Steve shared what it takes to be successful.
"I'm convinced that about half of what separates the successful **entrepreneurs** from the non-successful ones is pure perseverance."

What Is a Computer Innovator?

An innovator is a person who introduces new methods or procedures that change the way things are done. Being an innovator means being able to think creatively. Innovators are not afraid to try something, even if others think it will not work.

The world of computers is filled with innovators. Many computer innovators are scientists with training in engineering, electronics, chemistry, or physics. Others are untrained amateurs who are fascinated with computers and the way they work. Many innovators have contributed to the creation of computers today. However, no one person is solely responsible for an invention. Instead, people have continued to experiment and build upon ideas and technologies that have come before them.

SMARTPHONES

A smartphone is a cell phone that has extra features, including internet access. While smartphones perform the same function as a cell phone, most offer email, web browsing, video calling, music-playing, and still and video camera capabilities. The first smartphone was built by IBM in 1993 and was called the Simon Personal Communicator. However, the phone was too expensive and heavy to be widely used. A more practical smartphone was finally created 10 years later. It was small and powerful enough for everyday use.

Computer Innovators 101

Bill Hewlett and David Packard
(1913–2001)   (1912–1996)

Bill Hewlett and David Packard met in the early 1930s, when they were both studying at Stanford University in California. In 1939, Bill and David started the electronics company Hewlett–Packard (HP) in Packard's garage in Palo Alto, California. The company is recognized as establishing the area known as Silicon Valley. Today, HP is one of the biggest computer companies in the world.

Konrad Zuse
(1910–1995)

Konrad Zuse was a German **engineer** who developed the first programmable computer, the Z3, in 1941. The program that ran the computer was on a long paper tape punched with holes. Konrad could change the function of the computer by changing the holes in the tape, something that had never been seen before. These computers were used to design missiles and other weapons in World War II.

Henry Edward Roberts
(1941–2010)

Ed Roberts is considered by the industry to be the father of the personal computer. In 1969, Ed founded Micro Instrumentation and Telemetry Systems (MITS). He designed and helped construct the first commercially available personal computer, the Altair 8800, in 1975. In 1977, Ed sold MITS to Pertec Computer Corporation for about $6 million. He then decided to enter the medical field, becoming a doctor in 1986.

Bill Gates
(1955–)

Bill Gates is the co–founder of Microsoft Corporation, one of the biggest computer companies in the world. In 1975, Bill and Paul Allen, a childhood friend, began making software for an Altair microprocessor. By 1978, Microsoft's annual sales were in excess of $1 million. Today, Bill is considered one of the wealthiest people in the world. He has given billions of dollars to charity through his Bill and Melinda Gates Foundation.

Influences

Bill Hewlett was the president of HP from 1964 to 1977.

Steve was only 12 years old when he was offered a summer job at HP.

Steve credited his teachers as influences in his life. One teacher who took early note of Steve's interest in technology was John McCollum. He taught electronics. Under Mr. McCollum's guidance, Steve was soon building different types of electronic devices.

One week, Mr. McCollum gave Steve a homework project. To complete the project, Steve needed spare parts. He called a local company to see if it had what he needed. That local company was Hewlett-Packard. Steve ended up speaking to Bill Hewlett himself. Mr. McCollum was shocked, especially when he learned that Steve had been given a summer job out of the meeting.

Steve also gained knowledge and inspiration from his time as a member of the Homebrew Computer Club. The group met at California's Stanford University and discussed personal computers and electronics. Steve spent hours exchanging ideas and tips for constructing do-it-yourself computer kits. The knowledge he gained from the other members inspired him to build Apple years later.

THE JOBS FAMILY

In the 1990s, Steve met Laurene Powell at Stanford business school, where Laurene was studying. Steve was supposed to attend a business meeting, but instead took Laurene on their first date. The two were married on March 18, 1991. Together, they had three children, a son, Reed, and two daughters, Erin and Eve. Steve had another daughter, Lisa, from a previous relationship.

Overcoming Obstacles

When starting out, Steve and Apple had to deal with competition from big companies. In 1976, Steve was at the Personal Computer Festival in Atlantic City trying to sell his Apple I computer. His stand was next to one from a much larger company. It had salespeople in business suits, music, and dancers. Steve looked like an amateur next to them. However, he did not get upset. Instead, Steve used the situation to learn about the value of promotion and marketing. He went home and began taking steps to make Apple a more **professional** company.

Between 1997 and 2011, Steve would get on stage multiple times a year to introduce new Apple products to consumers.

Despite Apple's success, Steve disagreed with the company's **board of directors** on how the company should be run. In 1985, he agreed to step down as chairman and leave the company.

It was a tough time for Steve, but his creative spirit was never crushed. He bought Pixar and formed another computer company, called NeXT. In 1996, Apple bought NeXT, and Steve returned to his former company. He became its chief executive officer the following year.

Released on November 22, 1995, *Toy Story* was the world's first computer animated feature film.

In October 2003, Steve was diagnosed with pancreatic cancer. He had the cancerous tumor removed in July 2004, but his health remained a problem. In 2009, he had to return to the hospital for a liver transplant. Health problems again caused Steve to miss time at work in January 2011. Even though he had to take time away for treatment, he continued to work with Apple and promote its products.

Achievements and Successes

S teve Jobs continued to create and develop new technologies throughout his career. In 2001, Steve and his team at Apple introduced the iPod, a portable music device. The iPod was used to store and play music files that had been **downloaded** from the internet. Apple introduced the iPhone in 2007. This **multi-touch** telephone allows people to make phone calls, listen to music, surf the internet, and even watch movies. In 2010, Apple launched the iPad. The iPad offers a range of **applications** that allow the user to do everything from play games and read books to navigate the globe with mapping tools.

Steve helped launch the first iPhone in 2007. More than 2 billion iPhones have been sold since then.

Innovation is an important part of Apple's success. Steve and the team at Apple continued to improve on the design and technology of their products. Apple regularly introduces newer versions of the iPod, iPad, and iPhone. On October 5, 2011, the day after Apple introduced the iPhone 4S, Steve Jobs passed away following his long battle with cancer.

Steve received many awards and honors for his innovative thinking. In 2007, he was inducted into the California Hall of Fame. That same year, *Fortune* magazine named him the most powerful person in the world of business. Following his death, Steve was awarded a Grammy Trustees Award in recognition of the affect that the iPod and iTunes had on the music industry. Steve's influence is still felt in the continued success of the many Apple products that he helped introduce to the world.

HELPING OTHERS

During his lifetime, Steve Jobs never publicly announced his donations to charity. He believed that the products that were being created by Apple would be a more lasting contribution to help people live better lives. Following his death, it was revealed the Jobs family donated more than $50 million to hospitals in California. This money was put towards building a children's medical center. Steve also contributed to AIDS charities and HIV research.

Write a Biography

A person's life story can be the subject of a book. This kind of book is called a biography. Biographies describe the lives of remarkable people, such as those who have achieved great success or taken important actions to help others. These people may be alive today, or they may have lived many years ago. Reading a biography can help you learn more about a remarkable person.

At school, you might be asked to write a biography. First, decide who you want to write about. You can choose a computer innovator, such as Steve Jobs, or any other person. Then, find out if your library has any resources about this person. Learn as much as you can about him or her. Write down the key events in this person's life. What was this person's childhood like? What has he or she accomplished? What are his or her goals? What makes this person special or unusual?

A concept web is a useful research tool. Read the questions in the following concept web. Answer the questions in your notebook. Your answers will help you write a biography.

Adulthood

- Where does this individual currently reside?
- Does he or she have a family?

Your Opinion

- What did you learn from your research?
- Would you suggest these resources to others?
- Was anything missing from these resources?

Childhood

- Where and when was this person born?
- Describe his or her parents, siblings, and friends.
- Did this person grow up in unusual circumstances?

Writing a  Biography

Work and Preparation

- What was this person's education?
- What was his or her work experience?
- How does this person work? What is or was the process he or she uses or used?

Main Accomplishments

- What is this person's life's work?
- Has he or she received awards or recognition for accomplishments?
- How have this person's accomplishments served others?

Help and Obstacles

- Did this individual have a positive attitude?
- Did he or she receive help from others?
- Did this person have a mentor?
- Did this person face any hardships? If so, how were the hardships overcome?

Steve Jobs Timeline

Steve Jobs Events		World Events
Steven Paul Jobs is born on February 24.	**1955**	Albert Einstein dies on April 18.
Steve and Stephen Wozniak launch Apple Inc. on April 1.	**1976**	Bill Gates and Paul Allen register Microsoft as the name of their new company.
Steve resigns from Apple.	**1985**	The first internet **domain name** is registered.
Steve buys Pixar Animation Studios.	**1986**	Fuji introduces the first disposable camera.
Steve becomes chief executive officer of Apple for the second time.	**1997**	IBM's Deep Blue computer defeats chess champion Garry Kasparov for the first time.
Steve dies of cancer on October 5 in his California home.	**2011**	The world population reaches an estimated 7 billion in October, according to the United Nations.
Apple becomes the first company in the United States to be worth $3 trillion.	**2022**	The first successful transplant of a pig's heart into a human body occurs in Baltimore, Maryland.

Key Words

adopted: taken into one's family through legal means and raised as one's own child

applications: computer software designed to help the user perform specific tasks

board of directors: a group of people elected to manage a company or organization

chief executive officer (CEO): the highest ranking manager or administrator in a company

circuit board: the panel on which a computer's components are connected

domain name: a name owned by a person or organization and used as an internet address

downloaded: saved to a computer, often from the internet

engineer: a highly skilled technician or scientist who develops ways and devices to make things work

entrepreneurs: people who create and take responsibility for a new company, invention, or idea

high-resolution graphics: images that can be seen vividly and printed clearly

innovations: new ways of thinking or doing something

logo: a symbol used to represent a company

marketing campaign: a series of activities used to advertise a product or service

microprocessor: a chip that contains a circuit of electrical components that can process programs, remember information, and perform calculations

multi-touch: the ability for a touch-screen device to register several touches at once

professional: having businesslike standards and conduct

Index

Get the best of both worlds.

AV2 bridges the gap between print and digital.

The expandable resources toolbar enables quick access to content including **videos**, **audio**, **activities**, **weblinks**, **slideshows**, **quizzes**, and **key words**.

Animated videos make static images come alive.

Resource icons on each page help readers to further **explore key concepts**.

Published by Lightbox Learning Inc.
276 5th Avenue
Suite 704 #917
New York, NY 10001
Website: www.openlightbox.com

Library of Congress Cataloging-in-Publication Data
Names: Goldsworthy, Steve, author.
Title: Steve Jobs / Steve Goldsworthy.
Description: New York, NY : Lightbox Learning, [2023] | Series: History makers. Past and present | Includes index. | Audience: Grades 4-6.
Identifiers: LCCN 2022001779 (print) | LCCN 2022001780 (ebook) | ISBN 9781791146313 (library binding) | ISBN 9781791146320 (paperback) | ISBN 9781791146337 (ebook)
Subjects: LCSH: Jobs, Steve, 1955-2011--Juvenile literature. | Computer engineers--United States--Biography. | Inventors--United States--Biography--Juvenile literature. | Businesspeople--United States--Biography. | Apple Computer, Inc.--History--Juvenile literature.
Classification: LCC QA76.2.J63 G65 2023 (print) | LCC QA76.2.J63 (ebook) | DDC 338.7/61004092 [B]--dc23/eng/20220128
LC record available at https://lccn.loc.gov/2022001779
LC ebook record available at https://lccn.loc.gov/2022001780

Printed in Guangzhou, China
1 2 3 4 5 6 7 8 9 0 26 25 24 23 22

022022
101121

Project Coordinator: Heather Kissock
Designer: Terry Paulhus

Photo Credits
Every reasonable effort has been made to trace ownership and to obtain permission to reprint copyright material. The publisher would be pleased to have any errors or omissions brought to its attention so that they may be corrected in subsequent printings. The publisher acknowledges Alamy, Getty Images, Shutterstock, Hewlett-Packard, and Wikimedia as its primary image suppliers for this title.

View our titles and product videos at www.openlightbox.com